By the Sea

by Dick Martin
illustrated by Judith Pfeiffer

HOUGHTON MIFFLIN BOSTON

Printed in China

ISBN-13: 978-0-547-01721-1
ISBN-10: 0-547-01721-9

3 4 5 6 7 8 9 0940 15 14 13 12 11 10

We will see some things
by the sea.

We will see some fish
by the sea.

We will see some snails
by the sea.

We will see a starfish
by the sea.

We will see seaweed
by the sea.

We will see an octopus
by the sea.

We will see a crab
by the sea.

Look! Look!

We will see . . .

. . . a whale in the sea!

Responding

TARGET SKILL **Author's Purpose** Why did the author write this book? Make a chart. Tell three things you learned about the sea.

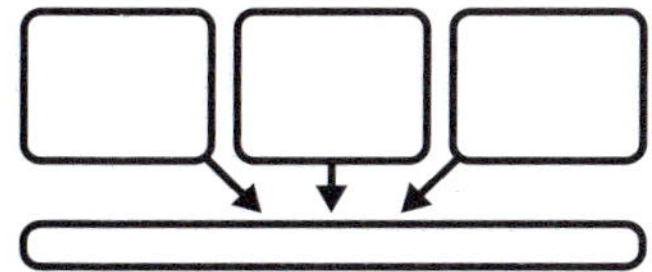

Write About It

Text to World Draw a picture of things you can see by the sea. Write a letter to a friend. Tell about your picture.

WORDS TO KNOW

be	will

LEARN MORE WORDS

octopus	starfish

TARGET SKILL **Author's Purpose**

Tell why an author writes a book.

TARGET STRATEGY **Analyze/Evaluate**

Tell how you feel about the text, and why.

GENRE **Informational text** gives facts about a topic.